A Fish Named Matroly

(muh-trow-lee)

By Dianne Gremillion

Global Book Publishers/Charleston, SC

Booksurge.com

This book is
lovingly dedicated
to
my wonderful nieces & nephews ~
Brent, Ellen, Lauren, Andrew, Zachary, Jared, Cameron,
Cade, Caleb & Kelcie!

Matroly's name is a "fruit-of-the-spirit" ~Christened so by Zachary
Who proudly learned The "fruits-of-the-spirit"
As "yub, joy, pashunts and self-matroly!"

Global Book Publishers/Charleston, SC
Order from: Booksurge.com
Illustrated by: Dianne Gremillion and Brenda Cravens
Cravenart@lowcountry.com or matroly@aol.com
Printed in the United States of America

This is Matroly.

He lived in a tiny cup on the shelf of a store.

Every day Matroly swam in circles flaunting his feathery gills while people admired him through the shop window.

At night Matroly lay in his cup wishing he had a friend to play with. Matroly felt cramped in the cup and dreamed of having a home all his own.

Finally the day came when a bright-eyed blonde haired boy named Zachary stopped in front of the cup Matroly called home.

"Oh look!" shouted Zachary, "he's the prettiest fish here! And I think he's smiling at me."

Matroly perked up. He swam three quick laps around his cup, looking over his shoulder to see whether the boy was still watching. Matroly ended the swim with a flourish of his feathery tail and cast a big grin at Zachary.

"Look Aunt Emilee!! He smiled at me again! Can we please take him home?"
Aunt Emilee agreed that Zachary could take Matroly home.

Aunt Emilee and Zachary spent the next hour picking out the perfect fish bowl for Matroly to live in. Zachary chose shiny blue and silver marbles to line the floor of Matroly's new home.

Aunt Emilee called her friend Andrew who knew everything there was to know about taking care of fish. Andrew came over to instruct Zachary how to take care of Matroly. "First you need to make the water special. Add this tablet to the water," he said.

Zachary made the water special just like Andrew told him to do. Then he placed a thermometer sticker on the side of Matroly's fish bowl. Matroly likes the water to be warm since he is a tropical fish.

Zachary and Aunt Emilee went back to the store to pick out some trees for Matroly. Andrew told them that Matroly would enjoy swimming around the trees. "And if he is happy, he will make a bubble nest." At last Matroly's new home was ready!

Matroly acted frightened when Zachary moved him from his cup palace to the new bowl. Zachary hoped Matroly would soon make a bubble nest. Matroly swam wildly back and forth.

He wanted to make bubbles and let Zachary know he was so happy to live here but he was feeling a little frightened. He had to adjust to his new environment.

Zachary looked sad. "It takes time for a fish to adjust to a new environment," Aunt Emilee told him. "He will be fine in a day or two."

As soon as Matroly felt at home in his bowl, he began to blow bubbles, big bubbles for Zachary to see that he was happy! Every day Zachary gave Matroly three pellets of fish food just like the directions said.

Zachary and Aunt Emilee took Matroly everywhere they went.....hiking in the redwood forest.

...taking a picnic at the beach....

Zachary even took him to school one day for show and tell!

Matroly grew and was very happy. He had found the perfect home ~

and a friend to play with! Matroly wonders ~would you like to have
a fish friend too?

the
end!

Made in the USA
San Bernardino, CA
25 January 2016